BIRDS

Cardinals

James E. Gerholdt
ABDO & Daughters

Published by Abdo & Daughters, 4940 Viking Drive, Suite 622, Edina, Minnesota 55435.

Copyright © 1997 by Abdo Consulting Group, Inc., Pentagon Tower, P.O. Box 36036, Minneapolis, Minnesota 55435 USA. International copyrights reserved in all countries. No part of this book may be reproduced in any form without written permission from the publisher.

Printed in the United States.

Cover and Interior Photo credits: Peter Arnold, Inc.

Edited by Julie Berg

Library of Congress Cataloging-in-Publication Data

Gerholdt, James E., 1943—
    Cardinals/James E. Gerholdt.
         p.   cm. -- (birds)
    Includes index.
    Summary: Describes the physical characteristics, habits, and natural habitat of
this brightly colored bird which can be easily identified by the crest on the top of its
head.
    ISBN 1-56239-585-8
    1. Northern cardinal--Juvenile literature. [1. Northern cardinal. 2. Cardinals (Birds)]
    I. Title. II. Series: Gerholdt, James E., 1943—Birds.
    QL696.P2438G47   1997
    598.8'83--dc20
                                         96-311
                                       CIP
                                       AC

Contents

NORTHERN CARDINALS

Northern cardinals belong to one of the 28 **orders** of **birds**. They are in the same **family** as sparrows and finches. They are known as cardinals because their bright red colors are the same as the robes worn by the cardinals of the Roman Catholic Church.

Birds are **vertebrates**. This means they have backbones just like humans. Birds are also **warm-blooded**.

Northern cardinals are a bird watcher's favorite. Their bright colors make them easy to see, and they often **perch** on backyard feeders. The sight of a northern cardinal outside your window is something to remember!

Sparrows (left) and cardinals are in the same bird family.

A male cardinal in the Arizona desert.

SIZES

Northern cardinals are medium-sized **birds**. The females and males are the same size. They weigh 1 1/4 to 2 ounces (35 to 53g).

From the tip of the beak to the tip of the tail, cardinals measure 7 1/2 to 8 1/2 inches (19.5 to 21.6cm). The **wingspan** is 10 1/4 to 12 inches (26 to 30.5cm).

Opposite page: A cardinal in flight showing its wingspan.

SHAPES

Northern cardinals are round-bodied, stocky **birds**. Their tails are long and rounded. Their beaks are heavy and triangle-shaped, and help them to eat seeds.

The pointed **crest** on the top of the head makes this bird easy to identify. The feet are made for **perching**, and have four toes—three in front, and one in back.

Opposite page: Cardinals have long tails.

COLORS

The male northern cardinal is one of the most beautiful **birds** you can find in your backyard. It is almost completely bright red, with a black patch of **feathers** around a red beak.

The female is a brown color, with some red on the wings and the tail. She also has the black patch around the red beak. The babies are much like the female in color, but their beaks are black.

A female cardinal.

A male cardinal.

WHERE THEY LIVE

Northern cardinals are found over much of the United States, as far west as California and Arizona. They also are found in Ontario and Quebec, in Canada, and range as far south as Belize in Central America. This **bird** has also been introduced into Hawaii.

The edges of woods, thickets, and gardens in towns and cities are where you will find cardinals. They are often attracted to backyard bird feeders. Northern cardinals seldom fly far from where they **hatched**.

Canada

United States

Central America

The cardinal is found from Canada through Central America.

12

Cardinal in a snow-covered white pine.

SENSES

Northern cardinals have the same five senses as humans. Their senses of taste and smell are not very good. But neither of these senses is very important to them.

The northern cardinals' eyesight is very good and helps them find food. The sense of hearing is also important. It helps them to locate an insect meal, and to hear the song of another cardinal. Most female birds don't sing. But all cardinals do sing. Their songs are the same, but the males' are louder.

Opposite page: Cardinals have good eyesight.

DEFENSE

The northern cardinal is a strong flyer, and can fly away from many of its **enemies** at 25 miles per hour (40 kilometers per hour).

The male cardinal will defend its **territory** against another male. It will even attack its reflection in glass windows and shiny hubcaps, which can hurt the **bird**.

Opposite page: A female cardinal in flight.

FOOD

Northern cardinals belong to the **order** of **birds** known as seedeaters. But they also eat other things. When this bird feeds, it hops along the ground or moves through trees and shrubs in search of a meal.

Many kinds of insects and spiders are eaten. Snails and slugs are also a favorite snack. Fruit, corn, oats, rice, and flowers are other items that are eaten by this bird.

If a northern cardinal finds a hole in a maple tree, it will drink the **sap**. In a backyard bird feeder, the cardinal likes sunflower seeds and cracked corn.

Opposite page: A cardinal walking along the ground looking for food.

BABIES

All northern cardinals **hatch** from eggs, which measure 1 by 3/4 inches (25 x 18mm). They are a pale blue or greenish white, or sometimes grey, with brown, purple, or grey blotches. Often, 3 to 4 eggs are laid at one time. But sometimes 2 or 5 are laid.

The nest is usually made by the female out of twigs, leaves, bark strips, and grass. This nest is built in a tree or dense shrubs 3 to 20 feet (1 to 6m) above the ground. The babies hatch after 12 or 13 days and leave the nest when they are 10 or 11 days old.

The adult male watches over the babies after they leave the nest.

Opposite page: Baby cardinals in a nest.

GLOSSARY

bird (BURD) - A feathered animal with a backbone whose front limbs are wings.

crest - A tuft or ridge, or other natural growth on the head of a bird.

enemy - Something dangerous or harmful to something else.

family (FAM-uh-lee) - A grouping of animals ranked lower than an order.

feather (FETH-ur) - The light, flat structures covering a bird's body.

hatch - To come forth or be born from an egg.

order (OAR-der) - A grouping of animals ranked higher than a family.

perch - Anything on which a bird can come to rest, such as a bar or branch. Also, the act of coming to rest.

sap - A liquid that flows through a plant or tree.

territory (TAIR-uh-tor-ee) - Any area of land held by someone or something.

vertebrate (VER-tuh-brit) - An animal with a backbone.

warm-blooded (warm-BLUD-ed) - Regulating body temperature at a constant level, from inside the body.

wingspan (WING-span) - The distance from the tip of one wing to the other.

INDEX